Bulletin Boards for All Occasions

Creative Ideas for the Congregation

by Carolyn Luetje

Augsburg Fortress, Minneapolis

Contents

Acknowledgments

Illustration: Berta Zimdars
Cover and page design: RKB Studios
Editors: Beth Ann Gaede, Louise Lystig

Scripture taken from the Holy Bible, New International Version®. Copyright © 1973, 1978, 1984 by International Bible Society. Used by permission of Zondervan Publishing House. All rights reserved.

The "NIV" and "New International Version" trademarks are registered in the United States Patent and Trademark Office by International Bible Society. Use of either trademark requires the permission of International Bible Society.

•••••••••••••••••••••••••••• Introduction

We see and react to visual messages every day. Billboards, greeting cards, magazines, and television ads all project or enhance their messages by incorporating pictures and symbols. Businesses, educators, family members, and friends communicate more effectively with us through visual messages.

Such messages are important in our congregational life. When we see symbols such as the manger, the dove, and the cross, we immediately think of the biblical events they represent. Religious symbols and pictures hold deep meaning for us and appear in works of art, in stained glass windows, on jewelry, altar cloths, and pastors' stoles. Christians often communicate their faith to others not only through words but through visual messages.

You can communicate with members and friends of your congregation by creating colorful, inviting bulletin boards. This book offers guidelines and ideas to use in creating bulletin boards for your congregation. Eye-catching displays will help you hold attention, present information, and encourage participation in congregational activities. They also will let people know that your congregation is alive, enthusiastic, and involved.

Bulletin boards offer an ideal way for the church governing body, committees, and organizations to inform the congregation about their activities. Youth groups can use bulletin boards to announce upcoming events and encourage participation. Sunday school classes can display current or ongoing projects. Bulletin boards also can be used to help members of the congregation learn about each other, to welcome new members and visitors, and to announce banquets, retreats, and other events. Use this book as a springboard for your own creativity and imagination; feel free to change or adapt the ideas to meet your own needs.

•••••••••••••••••••••• Determining Your Purpose

The first step in creating a bulletin board is to decide on the purpose of your bulletin board. Before you plan your display, think about what you are trying to accomplish. Do you want to . . .

- present information?
- announce a special event?
- ask for help?
- encourage involvement?
- create interest in church activities?
- celebrate seasons of the church year or the calendar year?
- welcome visitors or new members?
- share the Christian faith with others?

It is important to be clear about the purpose of your bulletin board because what you want to accomplish will influence what you display and how you display it. For example, if you wish to celebrate church festivals or seasons, you will probably display symbols associated with those occasions. To pass on information to the congregation from its leaders, however, you will probably use fewer visuals and more written material.

Think also about the people you wish to reach. Are you trying, through your bulletin board, to communicate with members? visitors? adults? youth? children? all ages? The age and make-up of your audience will determine, to a large extent, what you put on the bulletin board. For example, if you are designing a bulletin board for children, you would use mostly pictures or other visuals, while a bulletin board for adults could have fewer pictures and more words and titles.

If you have more than one bulletin board in your church, try to set up your display on a board that will be seen easily by your intended audience. You will want to put invitations and information for visitors near main entrances, while promotion for the next youth group outing probably belongs next to the room where the high school Sunday school class meets.

Designing Your Bulletin Board

Once you have decided what you are trying to accomplish and whom you wish to reach, it is time to design your bulletin board. Think about bulletin boards you have seen. Did some intrigue you and invite you to find out more? Were others easy to pass by without a second glance? What made the difference? Keep these ideas in mind as you plan your bulletin board.

Visual effect

Bulletin boards are primarily visual. Visual images stay in our minds long after words fade from our memories. Words and titles are important, and they should complement but not dominate the visual effects you create.

Theme

A bulletin board should revolve around one central idea. Decide on a single, unifying theme for your bulletin board, and then make sure everything you include enhances that theme.

Color

God created a world full of color for us to appreciate and enjoy. Two or three bright, coordinated colors make bulletin board displays attractive and appealing.

Balance

Our eyes and our minds seek and appreciate balance. You can achieve formal balance by placing items on the bulletin board in a symmetrical arrangement. Or you can balance items in an informal, nonsymmetrical way.

Simplicity

A simple, uncluttered bulletin board will be more effective than one that is complicated and busy. Use large, clear visuals and make words and titles short and easy to understand.

Organizing Supplies

When you begin to work on your bulletin board, you will need certain basic supplies. Here are some items you might want to keep on hand:

A variety of types and colors of paper

Sharp scissors

Stapler and staples

Straight pins, thumbtacks, or push pins

A variety of tapes and adhesives such as transparent tape, masking tape, package tape, white glue, wall mounting tabs, adhesive putty

Felt-tip markers, crayons, pencils, paint

Magazines, catalogs, greeting cards, coloring books, stencils, and other sources for pictures

Border patterns (see pages 7-9)

Letter patterns (see pages 45-48)

Store bulletin board supplies together in an easily accessible location so that you can quickly find what you need. You may wish to store small items together in a plastic storage caddy or desk organizer.

Choosing Bulletin Board Backgrounds

To make your bulletin board more attractive, cover with a bright, inviting background. Colored construction paper, plain shelf paper, butcher paper, and colored poster board often are used for bulletin board backgrounds. Here are other possibilities to consider; you may wish to collect some of these materials in advance so they will be on hand when you need them.

Colored tissue paper

Patterned shelf paper

Plain or patterned gift wrap

Fabric (burlap, denim, felt)

Fabric scraps arranged in patchwork-fashion

Maps

Travel posters (available from travel agents)

Wallpaper

Paper tablecloths or place mats

Fish net

Colored freezer wrap

Aluminum foil

Magazine pages

Old calendar pages

Increase interest in your bulletin board displays by inviting others to help create them. Ask various groups—Sunday school classes, Bible study groups, committees, youth groups, senior citizens, and others—to make bulletin board backgrounds. Encourage groups to use their own ideas or choose one of the techniques described on the next page.

Wrap the completed backgrounds around long cardboard tubes and store with other bulletin board supplies until needed. When you are ready to create your bulletin board, select a background, cut it to size, and carefully tack or staple it onto the bulletin board. Take care to avoid wrinkles or creases.

Crayon resist

Press firmly on crayons to draw stripes or simple designs on plain shelf paper or butcher paper. Then paint the entire paper with watercolors or diluted tempera paint. The paint will adhere to the uncolored areas while beading up on the crayoned areas to create an interesting effect.

Tissue paper collage

Brush a thin layer of liquid starch or diluted white glue on plain shelf paper or butcher paper. Lay overlapping tissue paper scraps on top and let dry to create a collage effect.

Cookie cutter prints

Dip cookie cutters into shallow trays of tempera paint, and then press the cookie cutters gently onto a plain paper tablecloth. Select cookie cutters that coordinate with the theme of the bulletin board.

Finger paint

Pour puddles of several colors of liquid tempera paint onto plain shelf paper or butcher paper. Gently spread the paint with your hands, mixing colors and making lines, swirls, and other designs.

Marble painting

Dip marbles into shallow trays of liquid tempera paint, and then roll the marbles across plain shelf paper or butcher paper.

Rubbings

Use double-sided tape to fasten leaves, cardboard hearts, or other shapes to a table. Lay a sheet of plain shelf paper or butcher paper on top, and tape the sheet securely to the table. Rub back and forth over the shapes with the sides of unwrapped crayons.

Adding Borders

The next step, after selecting and putting up the background, is to add a border. A border will set off your bulletin board and give it a finished look by accenting or framing the board.

You can make your own borders from narrow strips of construction paper. Make a permanent, reusable border pattern by drawing a series of scallops, semicircles, or other shapes on poster board. Staple several strips of paper together. Cut out the poster board pattern, and use it to trace the border onto the top sheet of paper. Then carefully cut through all layers.

Consider framing your bulletin board with corner designs rather than borders that go all the way around the board. Make poster board patterns for easier tracing and cut several sheets of paper at once.

Clip-art books, available at art supply stores, are a good source of border and corner patterns. Use an opaque or overhead projector to project and enlarge patterns you choose. (See page 10 for directions on how to use an opaque or an overhead projector.)

Ready-made borders are available from stores that specialize in school, art and craft, or office supplies. Borders come in a wide range of solid colors, prints, and patterns. Most are about 2½ inches wide and are made of sturdy corrugated paper.

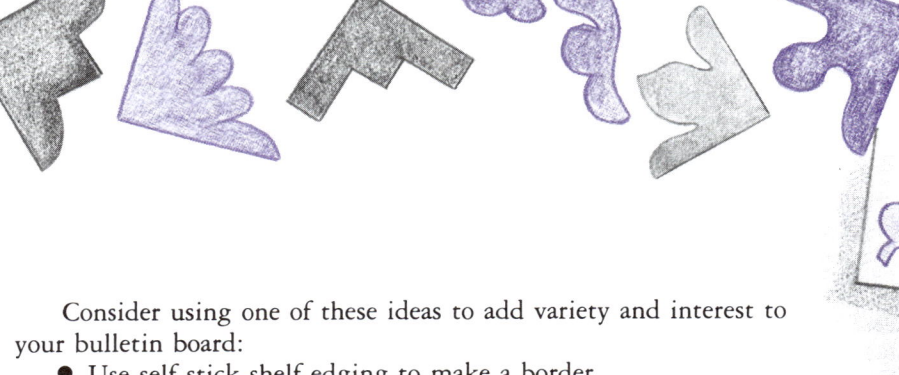

Consider using one of these ideas to add variety and interest to your bulletin board:

- Use self-stick shelf edging to make a border.
- Make a winter snowflake border by stapling paper doilies around the edges of the board.
- For Valentine's Day, staple a paper heart in the center of each doily in your winter snowflake border.
- Staple real or paper leaves onto your board for an autumn border.
- Create seasonal borders by cutting them from gift wrap.
- Use pinking shears or scallop-edged scissors to cut out paper borders.
- Put a border only at the top, bottom, or sides of the bulletin board. For example, tack pine boughs along the top of a winter board. Fringe a strip of green construction paper "grass" and staple it to the bottom of the board. Glue sand on a strip of paper, and cut out a "beach" to be stapled along the bottom of the board. Or drape several long crepe paper strips across the top and sides of the board.

Get congregation members involved by encouraging individuals or groups to create borders using one of the following methods.

Fabric collage

Brush white glue onto narrow poster board strips. Cover the glue with overlapping fabric scraps.

Sponge printing

Use a symbol, such as a star, butterfly, or lily, to make borders that represent seasons or events in the church year. Cut the symbol from a sponge, then dip the sponge in liquid tempera paint and print the design on narrow strips of construction paper.

Paper chains

Children love making paper chains, which make interesting bulletin board borders. Invite Sunday school classes to make bright construction paper chains.

Handprints

Place open palms in liquid tempera paint and make handprints on strips of plain paper.

Finding Visuals ●●●●●●●●●●●●●●●●●●●●●●●●●●

Now that your bulletin board is framed and ready, you can select pictures or objects to display. You can cut visuals for your bulletin board from magazines, catalogs, newspapers, church bulletin covers, calendars, greeting cards, coloring books, and clip-art books. You also can enlarge clip-art pictures, borders, and alphabet letters by using an opaque or overhead projector.

Opaque projector

To use the opaque projector, lay the picture on the machine and project it onto paper that you have taped to the wall. Move the projector backward and forward to obtain the size of image you want. Trace the lines with a pencil, color the image with markers, chalk, or crayons, and then cut the image out.

Overhead projector

To use an overhead projector, first make a transparency by laying a clear acetate sheet on top of your picture and tracing it with a fine felt-tip marker. Lay the transparency on the overhead projector and project it onto paper that you have taped to the wall. Trace the lines with a pencil, color the picture with markers, chalk, or crayons, and then cut it out.

To make figures last longer, cut them from poster board or tagboard and color them with markers or paint them with tempera or watercolors. To preserve your figures further, use a laminating machine to laminate them, or cover them with a clear adhesive plastic. The plastic coating will protect the figures and produce an attractive glossy finish.

Do not limit yourself to using only pictures or poster board figures. Many small objects can be attached to a bulletin board to make an eye-catching, three-dimensional display. Here are a few possibilities to spark your own creativity:

Leaves	Gloves	Lace
Pinecones	Mittens	Braid
Branches	Scarves	Yarn
Dried flowers	Hats	Ribbons
Feathers	Neckties	Jewelry

You can staple small or lightweight objects directly onto the bulletin board, or hang them using heavy-duty thread or fishing line that you have tacked on the upper frame of the board.

Make your bulletin board more attractive by mounting pictures before displaying them. Here are some suggestions:

- Tape or glue one or more pictures to a larger sheet of colored construction paper, gift wrap, or other paper. For variety, cut construction paper into large, theme-related shapes such as flowers, hearts, or leaves. Then mount a picture on each shape.
- Cut a frame or mat from colored construction paper or poster board and tape the picture behind it.
- Cut a frame from cardboard and make a fabric collage on it. See "Fabric Collage" on page 7 for directions.
- For three-dimensional frames, trim pictures to fit inside shallow box lids or cut pictures into circles and mount on colored paper plates.
- Cut curved or scalloped edges, tear uneven edges, or slightly burn or singe the edges of pictures before mounting or framing them.

Adding words ● ● ● ● ● ● ● ● ● ● ● ● ● ● ● ●

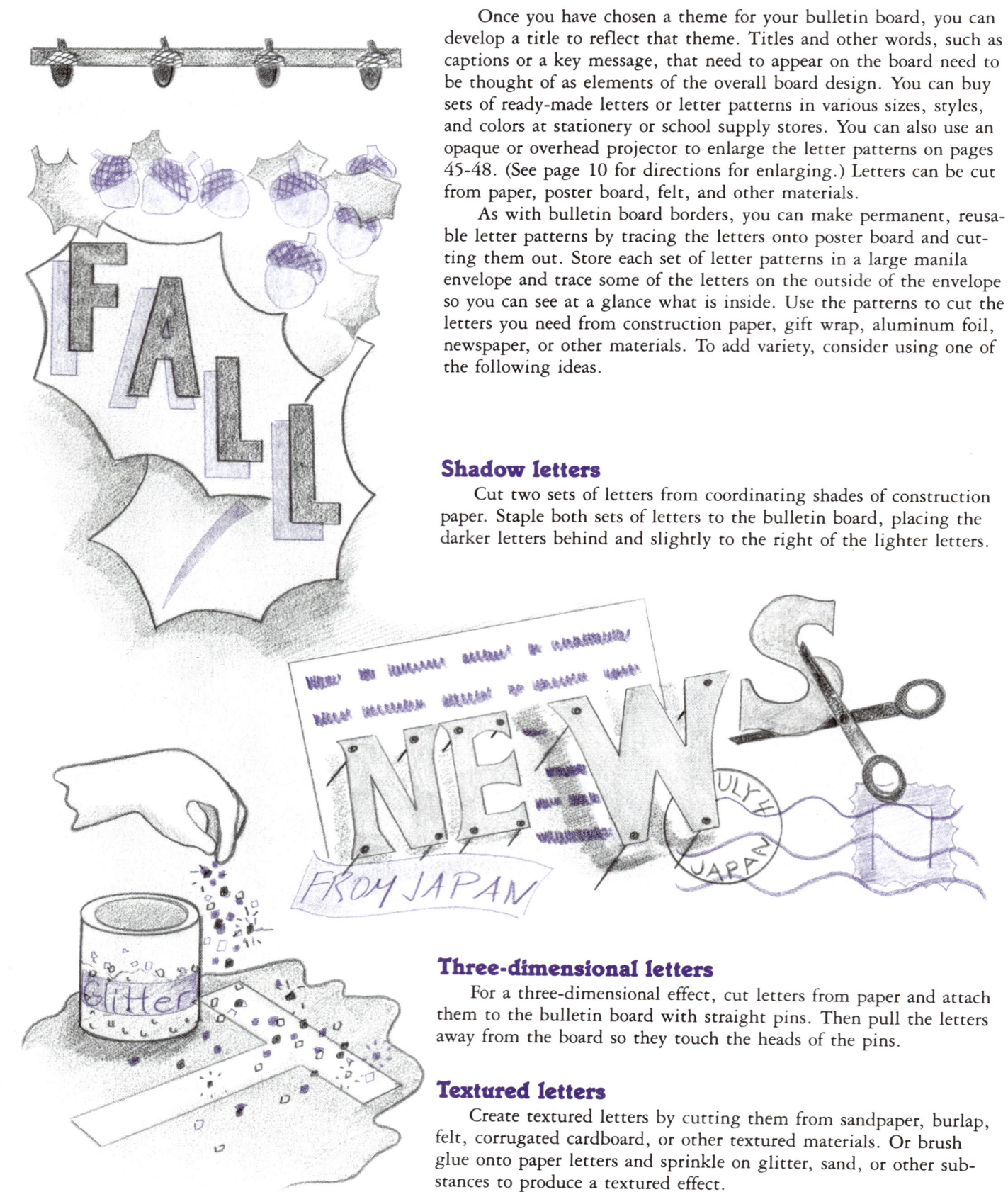

Once you have chosen a theme for your bulletin board, you can develop a title to reflect that theme. Titles and other words, such as captions or a key message, that need to appear on the board need to be thought of as elements of the overall board design. You can buy sets of ready-made letters or letter patterns in various sizes, styles, and colors at stationery or school supply stores. You can also use an opaque or overhead projector to enlarge the letter patterns on pages 45-48. (See page 10 for directions for enlarging.) Letters can be cut from paper, poster board, felt, and other materials.

As with bulletin board borders, you can make permanent, reusable letter patterns by tracing the letters onto poster board and cutting them out. Store each set of letter patterns in a large manila envelope and trace some of the letters on the outside of the envelope so you can see at a glance what is inside. Use the patterns to cut the letters you need from construction paper, gift wrap, aluminum foil, newspaper, or other materials. To add variety, consider using one of the following ideas.

Shadow letters

Cut two sets of letters from coordinating shades of construction paper. Staple both sets of letters to the bulletin board, placing the darker letters behind and slightly to the right of the lighter letters.

Three-dimensional letters

For a three-dimensional effect, cut letters from paper and attach them to the bulletin board with straight pins. Then pull the letters away from the board so they touch the heads of the pins.

Textured letters

Create textured letters by cutting them from sandpaper, burlap, felt, corrugated cardboard, or other textured materials. Or brush glue onto paper letters and sprinkle on glitter, sand, or other substances to produce a textured effect.

Write or print words on strips of white or colored paper and staple them to the bulletin board. If there is a skilled calligrapher in your congregation, consider asking that person to write some words or titles for you. If necessary, enlarge them on a copying machine.

Lightly sketch block letters on paper, then carefully tear the paper to form each letter. Or tear entire words from headlines in magazines or newspapers.

If you have access to a computer and printer, investigate the possibility of using it to produce words, titles, and graphics for your bulletin board. Many word processing programs offer a variety of typefaces and sizes.

After you have prepared your letters, place the words on the board, balancing them with the other design elements and making sure that the board will be attractive and easy to understand. As a rule, avoid arranging the letters of a word vertically, since that tends to be difficult to read.

Creating Alternate Display Areas

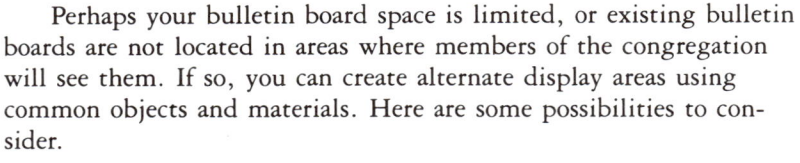

Perhaps your bulletin board space is limited, or existing bulletin boards are not located in areas where members of the congregation will see them. If so, you can create alternate display areas using common objects and materials. Here are some possibilities to consider.

Doors

Attach a background to a door using adhesives that will not damage the door's finish. Small adhesive tabs, available at school supply stores, hold materials securely without damaging most surfaces. Attach your bulletin board display to the background.

Walls and room dividers

Make a whole wall or a portion of a wall into a display area. Put up a background and frame it with a border. Again, be sure to use adhesives that will not damage the wall.

Windows

Windows make interesting display areas. You can tape simple shapes and letters to the glass or paint directly on the glass with acrylic or tempera paint. (Paint will wash off glass more easily if you mix the paint with dish soap before applying to the glass. Use about four parts paint to one part soap.)

Furniture

Consider using the sides or backs of large pieces of furniture, such as desks, pianos, or bookcases as display areas.

Portable bulletin boards

Make a portable bulletin board by placing a large piece of tagboard on an artist's easel or tripod. Use the tagboard as the background, and attach borders, visuals, and letters to it. Display your portable bulletin board where your intended audience will be most likely to see it.

Kiosk

To make a kiosk, obtain a large cardboard box or several cartons in graduated sizes. Paint the surfaces of each carton, or cover them with cloth, paper, wallpaper, or adhesive plastic. Stack the cartons, and attach visuals and announcements to all four surfaces of each carton. This type of display can be moved as needed.

Tabletop screen

Use three sides of a large carton, cut to a height of about 36 inches, to make a portable bulletin board. Paint the surfaces of the carton or cover them with paper, and then attach pictures, symbols, and announcements. Place the screen on a table in a hallway, the church narthex, the fellowship hall, or another convenient location.

Getting Started ●

Now you have the background information you need to begin creating inviting, eye-catching bulletin boards. Review suggestions on the previous pages as needed and be sure to use your own ideas and creativity. Ideas for bulletin boards are all around you—train yourself to scan advertisements, billboards, posters, and other sources for ideas you might be able to adapt for your purposes.

The next section offers a variety of bulletin board designs. You might find these helpful as you begin to collect your own ideas and materials. Several letter and border patterns are also included for your use. Use an overhead or opaque projector to enlarge the letters or visuals that follow to the size you need.

Holidays, Festivals, Seasons

Advent, which begins four Sundays before Christmas, is a time of preparation for the coming of Christ. Staple evergreen cuttings (or shredded green paper) to the bulletin board in an oval to make an Advent wreath. Add four blue (or three purple and one pink) paper or cardboard tubes for candles. Each Sunday, add an orange paper flame to one of the candles along with these explanations, printed attractively on separate sheets:

The prophets' candle (First Sunday in Advent) reminds us of the prophets who foretold Jesus' birth.

The Bethlehem candle (Second Sunday in Advent) reminds us of Jesus' birthplace.

The shepherds' candle (Third Sunday in Advent) reminds us of the shepherds who first heard the news of Jesus' birth.

The angels' candle (Fourth Sunday in Advent) reminds us of the angels who announced Jesus' birth.

Make your bulletin board look like a Christmas gift with red tissue paper background. Then divide the board into four sections with wide paper or fabric ribbons and a huge bow. In each section, post information about coming events such as an Advent festival, children's program, or choir concert. Present the information in a way that ties in with the gift theme, printing information on Christmas cards you make from construction paper or old cards. Or phrase the information using descriptions such as "the gift of music," and so on.

Dress up a Christmas bulletin board and recycle last year's Christmas cards. Look for cards with Christmas symbols such as a manger, a shepherd's crook, or an angel. Cover the board with plain red or green gift wrap. Make a border of ribbon and the fronts of the cards, and add bows at the top. Cut letters from contrasting gift wrap.

The poinsettia is used as a symbol of Christmas. To make these poinsettias, draw a 2-inch circle on a green or white background. Cut petals from red construction or tissue paper and glue them around the outer edge of the circle, overlapping the petals slightly. Brush glue over the circle and sprinkle on red or gold glitter.

Make a background for a Christmas bulletin board by printing with cookie cutters on red or green tissue paper. (See "Cookie Cutter Prints" on page 6.) Frame the board by stapling on candles made from painted cardboard gift-wrap tubes with orange construction paper flames. Add letters cut from Christmas gift wrap. Or make a nativity scene by cutting reusable figures from tagboard.

Gather cardboard tubes in a variety of lengths and paint them green. Then arrange them in the shape of a Christmas tree and glue them to a white background. Invite children to decorate the tree with snowflakes cut from folded paper, or ornaments made by covering 3-inch cardboard circles with colored foil.

Invite members of the congregation to greet one another with this giant Christmas card. Make a Christmas design on the front. Inside, write a Christmas greeting. Staple the card to the board, leaving the front of the card free. Hang colored markers along the sides of the board to encourage members and friends of the congregation to sign the card. Consider preparing several cards that could be delivered to homebound members or sent to a missionary supported by the congregation.

Use a pattern to cut angel shapes from 9-inch heavy paper circles. Invite children or youth to use crayons, markers, yarn, curling ribbon, glue, glitter, lace, and other materials to complete the angels. The children could present the angels to the congregation as a gift, possibly as part of a children's sermon about our role as God's messengers who proclaim the Christmas story. Write a Bible verse from the Christmas story on the bulletin board and arrange the angels around the words.

Welcome the New Year with a bright bulletin board featuring New Year's greetings. Staple or glue confetti, curling ribbon, and paper bells against a bright-colored background. Set up a table with shapes, markers, and tacks, and invite members of the congregation to write New Year's greetings on balloon-shaped pieces of construction paper and to sign their names, if they wish. Staple the balloons to the board and attach yarn or string to each one.

Epiphany, observed on January 6, is a celebration of the manifestation of Christ to the world. Begin this Epiphany bulletin board with a five-pointed construction paper star to represent the star of the East that led the Wise Men to Jesus. Three gold foil or construction paper crowns in the lower right corner symbolize the three Wise Men who brought their gifts to Jesus.

Observe Martin Luther King Jr. Day or President's Day with this bulletin board. Drop several dots of glue at random on the background, then sprinkle red or blue glitter on top. Brush on curving lines of glue radiating out from each glittered circle. Sprinkle glitter on the lines of glue to create exploding fireworks. Add photographs or drawings and significant documents. Complete the board with foil stars.

For Valentine's Day, cut round doilies in half and staple them side by side to form a lacy scallop border against a pink background. Cut out red paper hearts and on the back of each one, print a way to show love, such as: *bring canned goods for the food shelf; send a valentine; visit someone who is lonely.* Encourage children and adults to take a heart from the board and follow the suggestion on the back. Put up more hearts as needed.

Lent, the 40-day period preceding Easter, is a time of renewal and preparation for Easter. For this Lenten bulletin board, staple a construction paper road against a light-colored background, put people figures at the beginning of the road, and attach three tagboard crosses at the end of the road. Write traditional Lenten practices on tagboard signs and arrange them along the road.

World Day of Prayer is observed on the first Friday of March. Use this bulletin board to encourage the congregation to share prayer concerns. Cut small silhouettes of praying figures to put in the four corners of the board. Write directions for making prayer requests on the back of an envelope, place blank slips of paper inside the envelope, and tack it to the board, open side out.

If possible, use real palm branches to frame a bulletin board announcing Holy Week worship services. Palm branches have become symbols of Palm Sunday and its significance because the people of Jerusalem waved palms and laid them down before Jesus as he rode into Jerusalem. Palm branches also symbolize victory. Use purple, the color for Lent, for the background.

The Easter lily, which springs up from a dry, brown bulb, and the butterfly, which emerges from a lifeless-looking chrysalis, are common Easter symbols. Both have come to symbolize the new life we have because of Jesus' death and resurrection.

For many people, the cross is the most meaningful symbol of Jesus' death and resurrection. Create a living cross by stapling wire or plastic netting in the shape of a cross on the bulletin board and then inserting the stems of real or artificial flowers into the openings in the netting. Then invite children, youth, and adults to take a flower home as a reminder of the resurrection.

For this Easter bulletin board, tape together the long sides of four 12-inch-by-18-inch sheets of black construction paper. Fold over the sheets on each end so they meet at the center. Cut the shape shown in the illustration. To make the stained-glass windows, glue bright colored paper scraps on the closed shape. Cut bright yellow paper to fit inside, and write on it an Easter message. Staple the middle section to the board, leaving the front flaps free so they can be opened by viewers.

To make this Easter bulletin board, write the Bible verse on a sheet of butcher paper cut to fit the board. Brush glue on the lower portion of the paper, and then sprinkle on sand and add a paper fringe of grass. Mount the paper on the board. Attach a large tomb and a movable rock cut from grey or brown tagboard.

Collect the fronts of used Easter cards with a Christian theme, or ask youth to draw appropriate pictures for this Easter "quilt." Mount the cards or pictures on a pastel background, leaving room in the middle for an Easter greeting.

The celebration date for Arbor Day varies from state to state. For this bulletin board, cover an oatmeal container with bright adhesive paper, then tack the container to the board from the inside. Place a real or artificial tree branch through the lid of the container. Cut strips of flowered gift wrap for the border and cut letters from the same paper.

The dove is the most common symbol for the Holy Spirit. This choice is based on the biblical reference to the spirit of God descending in the form of a dove during the Baptism of Jesus (Matthew 3:16).

Make a large dove by enlarging and tracing the body and the wing onto heavy white paper. Cut out the pieces, glue white ornamental feathers to the wing, and staple both pieces to the bulletin board. Add details with markers.

The Trinity, or Pentecost, season begins on the Day of Pentecost and continues until the first Sunday in Advent. The dove and flames are both used as symbols for the season after Pentecost.

For this bulletin board, cut large paper flames from bright red or orange construction paper. Write the Bible verse on the flames, staple them to the bulletin board. If you wish, add a white paper dove.

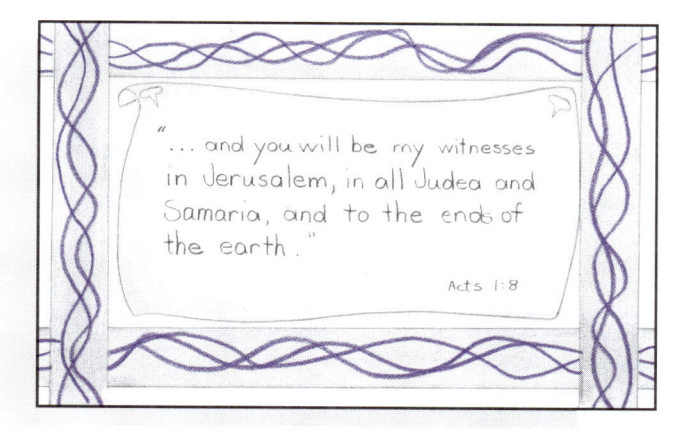

Before Jesus ascended into heaven, he promised his followers that they would receive the Holy Spirit and that they would be his messengers. Observe the Day of Ascension by framing a small bulletin board with wide bands of decorative woven braid. Write the Bible verse, using calligraphy or another decorative script, on parchment paper, and staple it between the bands of braid.

Invite members of the congregation to help create a Thanksgiving bulletin board. Display a large turkey shape, cut from brown wrapping paper, and arrange push pins on the turkey's body. Cut bright paper feathers and place them in an envelope that you have tacked to the board, open side out. Tie yarn or string around pencils and tack them to the board. Encourage children and adults to write down on paper feathers things for which they are thankful and pin the feathers to the turkey.

Organizations and Committees ·······················

Drape rope or heave-duty twine along the side of the bulletin board and staple or tack firmly in place. Ask congregational committees to write brief reports about issues they are currently considering. Mount committee reports on pennant shapes cut out of bright construction paper and clip to the rope with wooden spring-type clothespins. Place tack or tape on the underside of the pennants and press them to the board.

Use this bulletin board to invite the congregation to express opinions on questions being considered by the church governing body or committees. Draw one or two simple figures. Then draw balloons from the figures' mouths and write basic information inside the balloons. Include names and phone numbers of people members can call to give their opinions.

Bulletin boards that invite interaction can be a way to involve the congregation in decision making. For this bulletin board, display questions about issues your church council is considering. Staple two envelopes to the bulletin board, open side out. Place blank slips of paper in one, and label both envelopes. Tie yarn or string around pencils and tack to the board.

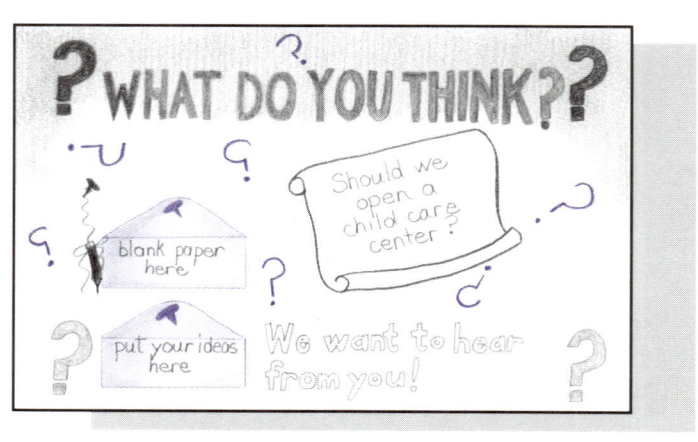

Invite congregational input with a suggestion box display. Remove the lid from an oatmeal container and cut a 3-inch-by-½-inch slit in it. Cover the container with attractive paper, write *suggestion box* on it, and tack the container to the bulletin board. Carefully replace the lid. Staple an envelope to the board, open side out, and place blank slips of paper inside. Tie yarn or string around pencils and tack them to the board.

Add interest to bulletin boards publicizing church organizations by decorating them with theme-related objects. For this bulletin board, use a plain fabric background and a jumbo rickrack border. Cut letters from a variety of patterned fabrics. Hang spools of thread from fishing line tacked to the top of the board.

Use this bulletin board to publicize activities of scout troops or other youth groups sponsored by your church. Ask group leaders to take a series of photographs of the children as they participate in a campout, a service project, or another activity. Then display the photos on the bulletin board, connected by paper footprints made by the children.

Announce church retreats with this bulletin board. Use real pine branches and needles or green and brown construction paper to make the trees that frame the board. Attach a brown construction paper cabin with doors that open and close. Write details about the retreat inside the cabin, behind the doors.

Let the congregation know about church-sponsored sports teams by hanging sports equipment or paper cut-outs of equipment from fishing line tacked to the top of the bulletin board. Use magazine or newspaper cutouts of athletes in action for the border.

Publicize fellowship opportunities by featuring a different congregation group each month. Drape dark red fabric across the top and down the sides of the board to resemble the curtains of an old-time theater. Title the board *Now Featuring* and add photos, labels, banners, and other objects related to the theme or purpose of the organization.

You might wish to establish a permanent bulletin board display to announce activities of various organizations within the congregation. Draw a theater marquee at the top of the board and add the caption *Coming Attractions.* Or use cardboard to create a marquee that projects over the board. Write information on paper strips and attach them below the marquee. Update the information on the board often.

Cut a winding brown paper path and staple it against a green background for a bulletin board that informs the congregation about organizations and their schedules. Use light-colored tagboard for the signpost and signs.

Use this bulletin board to encourage participation in environmental activities. Cut narrow bands of brightly colored paper for a top and side border. Attach real or paper cutouts of leaves, shells, or other natural objects. Attach paper strips with information about ways members and friends of the congregation can help care for creation.

Help members of the congregation find out more about church committees by putting up a "Committee of the Month" bulletin board. Collect a variety of shallow box lids and paint them with bright colors. Use the box lids as frames for photos of committee activities, reports of committee projects or responsibilities, and other information.

To promote interest in your church library, create a bulletin board with a hot-air balloon theme. Cut several large circles from heavy white paper, then invite a Sunday school class to collage them with bright-colored tissue paper (see page 6). You might also wish to ask a group of children to fingerpaint a sky blue background for the bulletin board. Staple the circles against the background, draw or attach strings, and staple on book jackets from books now available in your church library.

Each month, ask two or three committees to write a report of ideas they have been discussing and actions they have taken. Suggest they mount their reports on construction paper shapes that relate to their area of responsibility. For example, the music committee might mount their report on a musical note or the education committee might use a book-shaped background. Display the reports for the congregation.

Use the "help wanted" section of the newspaper as a background for this bulletin board publicizing the need for help with specific tasks on various committees or organizations. Write a "help wanted" ad for each position, following the format of those in the newspaper. Briefly describe skills that are needed and include names or phone numbers to call for more information.

Encourage members of the congregation to volunteer to serve on congregational committees with this bulletin board. Enlarge and trace a simple figure for the middle of the board, and surround it with phrases that describe the qualities that are needed.

Cut out and attach narrow strips of construction paper to frame announcements about organizations and their schedules. Pin shadow letters cut from contrasting paper inside the frame (see page 12). You might wish to leave the frame in place to use for other announcements.

This bulletin board will help members of the congregation understand how their benevolence contributions are helping others. Find out about ways your congregation's contributions for missions are used. Write a few sentences about each one and post it along with the title *You Are There!* Include photos, if possible.

Consider putting up a bulletin board that changes with the seasons. Announcements about congregational organizations and committees, reports from the church governing group or pastor, or information about congregational events can be mounted on coordinating construction paper and displayed next to the tree. You can also change the border to match the seasons.

You could begin with a bare tree in winter. Staple a brown paper tree trunk and branches against a light blue background. You can add Christmas decorations to the tree in December or attach paper snowflakes if you live in a snowy area.

In the spring, when the trees in your area begin to blossom or bud, invite a group of children to make handprint leaves for the tree. Provide shallow trays of tempera paint in colors of spring foliage in your area. Show the children how to dip gently their open palms in the green paint, and then press them onto a large sheet of butcher paper to make handprints. Encourage the children to keep working, overlapping the handprints, until the paper is covered. Cut out a large, leafy shape and staple it over the branches of the tree. If you want to make a flowering tree, crumple small squares of pastel tissue paper and glue them on top of the handprints.

In summer, make your tree resemble a fruit tree. Cut fruit from textured fabric or wallpaper. Or make apple prints by dipping apple halves or sponges cut in apple shapes in red tempera paint and printing apples on the tree. Thumbprint cherries can be made by having children dip their thumbs in red paint and make thumbprints on the tree.

In the fall, remove the green handprints and tissue-paper blossoms. Invite children to create a new set of handprint leaves, this time using autumn colors of red, yellow, orange, or brown. Or use real leaves that have been dipped in glycerin to preserve the colors.

If your congregation contributes to the support of a missionary family, consider a bulletin board similar to this one. Display a map of the country where your missionary family serves and mark the area where they work. You also could put up a world map with an inset map of the region the missionaries work in. Then display photos, letters, information, and small objects from that country.

Use this bulletin board to inform the congregation about missions your church supports. Cut sheets of construction paper to different lengths, then stack the sheets and staple to the board as shown. Write a question on the visible portion of each sheet. Display the answer to each question, along with photos and other information, on the hidden portion of the next sheet. Invite the congregation to life the flaps to find out the answers to the questions.

This bulletin board will enable you to display photos and other information about missions. Cover the display with a large sheet of heavy paper in which you have cut several openings. Position the information underneath so it will be only partially visible. Then attach the paper to the board, stapling along the top edge only. Invite the congregation to speculate on the information underneath, then lift the paper to find out the details.

The bulletin boards in this section are designed to help congregation staff and volunteer leaders communicate with others. These bulletin boards can be used to display reports and announcements from the congregation's governing body, pastor, and church organizations and committees. Use the bulletin boards over several weeks, posting new messages and notices often. Use a postmark date to let viewers know when the information was last updated.

For this bulletin board, display a mailbox, letters, and other mail-related items. Tack a large envelope to the board to hold a report from the church council or pastor.

Make church leaders' or pastors' reports stand out by mounting them on bright construction paper against a background of colorful fruit, flowers, or other shapes. Create the background by sponge printing (see page 8), by sketching simple shapes and painting them with watercolors, or by making a collage of magazine cutouts.

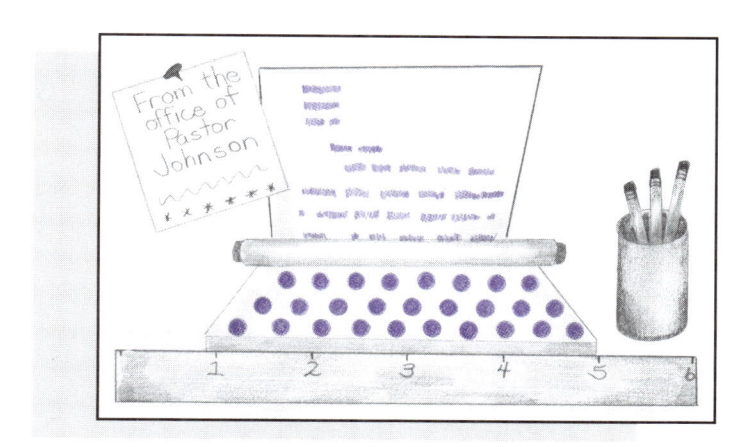

Use office supplies and other office-related items to decorate this bulletin board. Display your typed message above a picture of an oversized typewriter. Use large thumbtacks for the keys.

For this bulletin board, cut out a construction paper desk and common desktop objects, then tack them to the board. Attach pastor's announcements to the desk and write a title such as *From the Desk of Pastor Simpson* or *Notes from Pastor Nick*.

Use contrasting colors of construction paper to call attention to announcements from your pastor or church governing body. For example, staple alternating strips of red and white paper to the bulletin board. Use white letters to make words and titles stand out on the red paper, and black letters on the white paper.

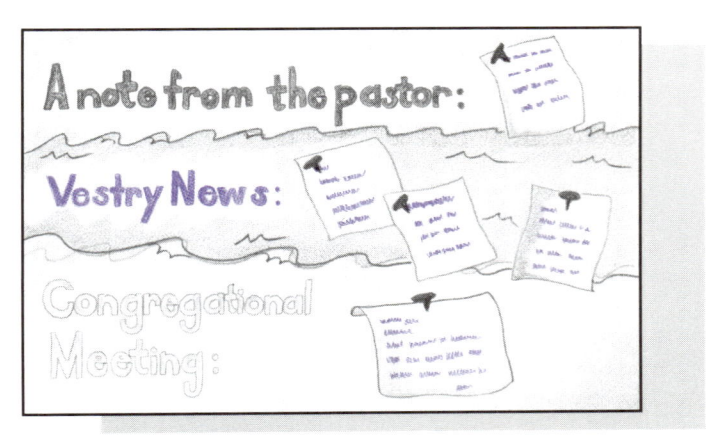

Make geometric shapes from interlocking strips of construction paper. Frame committees' or pastors' reports and post them inside the shapes.

Use a newspaper background for a bulletin board featuring news from your congregation's governing body or committees. Cut white paper to resemble an open book or newspaper and write information on it. Use a heavy black marker to write titles and draw illustrations.

Attach computer-produced reports and announcements to an oversized computer screen. If possible, use computer graphics to create a decorative border and titles.

You can use this bulletin board to keep the congregation up-to-date on what the congregation's governing body, committees, or organizations are doing. Attach a tagboard signpost over a newspaper background. Mount announcements on construction paper and hang from the sign.

For this bulletin board, use everybody's favorite means of communication—the telephone. Cut the telephone pieces from tagboard and connect them with real cord or string.

Congregational Events

Use a three-dimensional display to announce congregational dinners and other events. For example, cut out a large paper kettle and salad bowl. Attach dishes by stapling along the curved edges. Put a ladle, real or paper, inside the kettle. Tuck paper salad ingredients such as lettuce leaves, tomatoes, and shredded carrots inside the salad bowl.

Write information about congregational events on theme-related shapes. For this bulletin board, use bright paper kites and add string and fabric tails.

Use the colors of the sunrise to announce a morning Bible study, a breakfast meeting, or an Easter breakfast. Divide the bulletin board into thirds and cover the top section with yellow construction paper, the middle section with orange paper, and the bottom section with red paper. Attach a bright orange paper sun and white letters with blue shadows (see page 12).

Use a garden of tulips to announce spring events. Put up a pastel tissue paper background, and then fringe green construction paper to make a grass border. Write information on bright construction paper tulips.

Display clothing or other objects used by women of different generations or life-styles in the corners of the bulletin board to draw attention to announcements of women's activities. Write details on pastel paper and mount on a box-lid frame stapled to the middle of the board.

For a bulletin board about a food collection, staple on part of a cardboard carton or a paper grocery bag. Then tuck fronts of food cartons and canned goods labels inside the carton.

Tack tagboard signposts against a sky blue background and add a fringed "grass" border at the bottom of the bulletin board. Attach bright construction paper signs announcing summer activities.

A string of bright plastic or paper banners makes a good top border for a bulletin board announcing summer events. Carry out the theme by writing information on large paper banner shapes.

Perk up announcements of coming events with this bulletin board. Staple a 12-inch-by-18-inch sheet of bright construction paper against a background of randomly-arranged calendar pages. Write dates of next month's activities on a slightly smaller sheet of white paper, then mount the list on the construction paper.

Use a musical motif for announcements of musical events or rehearsal schedules for congregation musical groups. Draw a set of five horizontal black lines on a white background to resemble a staff. Add a treble clef and display information with black construction paper letters. You also may put black paper notes on the staff and print information below.

Pique curiosity with this three-dimensional bulletin board. Fold a sheet of 12-inch-by-18-inch construction paper in half to make a 9-inch-by-12-inch card. Write *You're Invited* on the front, below the fold, and write details of a congregational event inside. Staple the card to the board, leaving top flap free.

Planning a church picnic? Get the word out by stapling an empty potato chip bag, open end down, to the bulletin board. Write information on "potato chips" cut from manila or off-white construction paper.

Firmly tack the ends of a piece of rope or heavy twine at the upper left and right corners of the bulletin board so that the rope resembles a clothesline. Write information about a clothing drive on large paper clothes cutouts and glue or tape them to wire coat hangers. Hook the coat hangers over the clothesline.

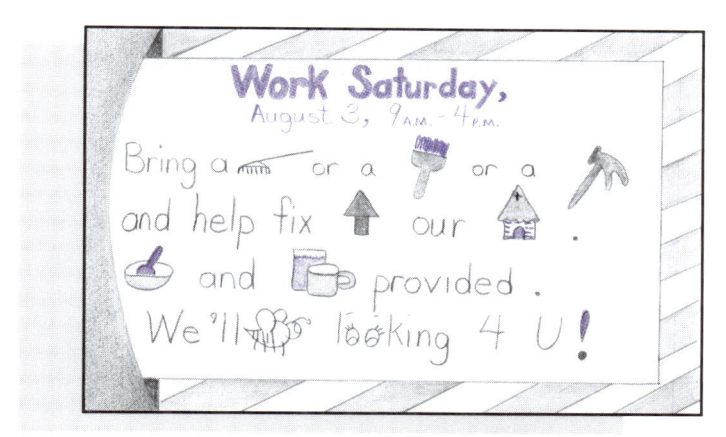

Challenge members of the congregation with a rebus message. Replace some of the words in an announcement of a congregational event with colorful stickers, magazine cutouts, or hand-drawn pictures.

For this bulletin board, invite a group of children to fingerprint a blue background. Suggest they use their fingers to make wavy lines in the paint to represent water. Then add a diving board, a diver (cut out from a magazine or drawn), and information about summer fun.

To announce fall events, staple a construction paper tree against a blue background. Make a border with small leaf shapes cut from orange, red, yellow, and brown construction paper, or staple on real leaves. You also could paint the backs of leaves, and before the paint dries, press the leaf veins on the background paper to make an imprint. Write information on larger leaf shapes.

Announce coming events by displaying construction paper cutouts that resemble your church sanctuary, fellowship hall, or other areas. Add information about the event and decorate the board with theme-related drawings or cutouts.

Use this bulletin board when you want members of the congregation to sign up for specific events. Make realistic-looking traffic signs and tack them to the board. Include a sign-up sheet, then tie yarn or string around pencils and tack them to the board.

For a "Welcome to the Family" bulletin board, use gift wrap with a baby-shower theme for the background. Make a border by tacking booties, rattles, bonnets, and other baby items along the sides. Add cutouts of baptismal symbols such as a shell or a baptismal font. Display photos of recently baptized babies and toddlers. Include children's names and names of family members.

Welcome newborn babies into the congregation with a bulletin board devoted just to them. Start with a background made from gift wrap that has a baby-shower theme. Then staple on part of cardboard carton and tuck shredded newspaper or excelsior inside. Write vital statistics for each newborn on a pastel tagboard card. Arrange the cards inside the carton.

Shells and water are used as symbols of Baptism. Commemorate Baptism anniversaries by hanging several large shells or stapling paper shell cutouts against a dark blue background. Tack light blue drops of water around the shells. Each month invite children, youth, and adults to write their names and Baptism date on the drops of water. Continue the bulletin board throughout the year so that all have an opportunity to participate.

Recognize young people who are being confirmed or celebrating their First Communion by displaying their class or individual pictures. Use real or artificial wheat and grapes as the border for this bulletin board. Cut shapes of a chalice and paten from tagboard and cover them with gold or silver foil. Place white construction paper wafers on the plate. You could use other shapes—a basket with a loaf of bread, for example—to reflect your own congregation's communion practices.

Make a bulletin board in a window that is visible from the street to reach out to the community. For example, tack brown tagboard strips against a white background to make the framework of an open window. Add fabric or paper curtains, and then write information about Bible study opportunities.

Almost everyone likes to be remembered on his or her birthday! Each month, write members' names and birthdates on 4-inch construction paper strips. Form each strip into a circle and staple to the board as shown to make a three-dimensional birthday cake. Then add a cardboard tube candle and paper flame. Or for large congregations, staple cupcake liners to the board, and insert paper cupcakes with a birthday name on each one. Be sure to change the bulletin board monthly.

This bulletin board will help people in the congregation become better acquainted. Invite individuals, families, or groups to take turns preparing the board. Suggest they display photos of themselves, pictures of their favorite foods, cutouts or objects related to their hobbies, and other items. Leave each display up two or three weeks. Encourage people to participate by placing a sign-up poster nearby.

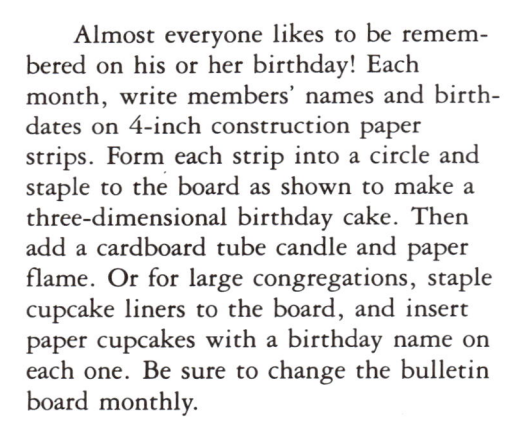

Reach out to the community with a bulletin board that provides information about your church's worship services and pastors. Cut a large door from brown construction paper and draw on a doorknob and other realistic details. Attach the door to the bulletin board by stapling along the left edge only. Behind the door, write the times of your worship services, the names and phone numbers of your pastors, and other information.

Celebrate cultural diversity with a multilingual bulletin board. Make a border with paper dolls cut from a variety of colors of construction paper, and be sure to include greetings in languages that are spoken in your community. For help with greetings in other languages, contact your local library or community college.

Use this bulletin board to celebrate family backgrounds as well as the idea that we are all part of the family of God. Staple a large blue circle, representing the earth, against a bright background. Cut out simple figures, each holding a flag (see illustration), and place them in an envelope you have tacked to the board, open side out. Invite members of the congregation to take a figure, decorate it to represent their own family background, and tack it to the board.

Mount photos of new members on seasonal shapes such as flowers or leaves. Include names, interests, and other information that will help the congregation get to know the new members.

Use a computer to create a large banner for this bulletin board. Add balloons, ribbons, or other designs with a computer graphics program. Attach the banner diagonally across the bulletin board, then complete the board by adding photos of new members.

Introduce and thank members of church groups with this bulletin board. Display photos of group members along with their names and a brief description of the group's activities and how members serve the church. Decorate the bulletin board with items related to the group's activities. Feature a different group each month.

For a "Get Acquainted" bulletin board, place small paper shapes in an envelope tacked to the board. On one Sunday, ask each person to decorate one side of a shape, write their name, address, and phone number on the other side, and pin the shape to the board with the decorated side out. The next Sunday, ask each one to take a shape from the board. Over the next few weeks, each person should anonymously get in touch several times with the person whose name they drew. On the last Sunday, ask "mystery messengers" to identify themselves and get to know one another.

A ticking watch can serve as a reminder of parish education opportunities. Mark the hours on a tagboard circle and attach movable tagboard hands with a paper fastener. Cut vinyl strips for the watchband. You might print *tick tock* and *It's time to . . .* directly on the background, then attach paper strips with additional information. Reuse the bulletin board for other reminders.

Use a bulletin board similar to this one to make members of the congregation aware of materials needed for Sunday school projects. Staple lightweight items directly on the board or hang them from heavy-duty thread or fishing line tacked to the top of the board. Nearby put a large basket or carton where people can put their donations.

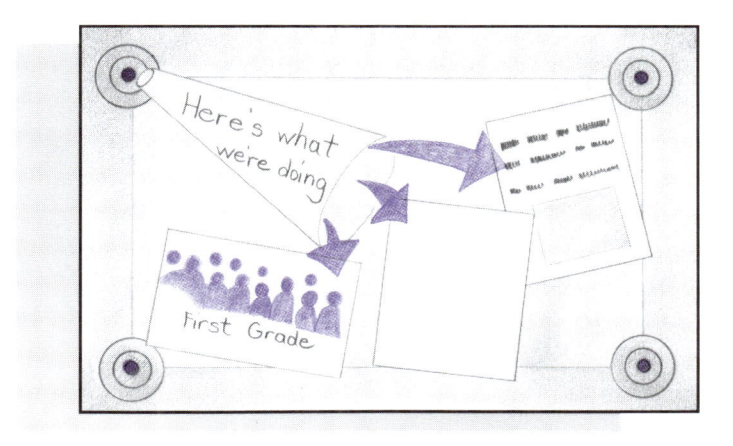

This bulletin board features a different Sunday school class each month. Invite classes to display artwork, photos, crafts, and other items they think will be of interest to the congregation. Encourage each class or teacher to design its own unusual and appealing bulletin board.

43

Draw bold arrows to call attention to announcements of adult Christian education classes. Mount a list of classes on construction paper and staple the list against a contrasting background.

Use that old summertime favorite—ice cream—as the theme of a bulletin board announcing schedules for summer Sunday school and vacation Bible school. Use paper ice cream cones to make side borders and cut letters from a rainbow of ice cream colors. You could put plastic foam balls (scoops of ice cream) in each cone.

Frame a bulletin board about parish education opportunities with balloons, hearts, and crayons. Add letters cut from bright construction paper and decorate with theme-related objects or cutouts.

Invite the congregation to a Sunday school activity with this bulletin board. Ask children to trace around their hands and feet, then cut out the paper shapes and write messages on them. Glue the cutouts to the bulletin board background, using them to make flowers and leaves in a garden mural.

Enlarge the following letter patterns to whatever size you want by using an opaque or an overhead projector (see page 10). Lightly trace letters onto tagboard or poster board. Cut letters out; then, if you wish, outline them. Place tape on the back of letters for reinforcement.

ABCDEFGHI

JKLMNOPQ

RSTUVWXY

Zabcdefghi

jklmnopqrs

tuvwxyz!?1

2345678 90

ABCDEFGHI
JKLMNOPQ
RSTUVWXY
Zabcdefghij
klmnopqrst
uvwxyz!?12
34567890

A B C D E F G H I J
K L M N O P Q R
S T U V W X Y Z
a b c d e f g h i j
k l m n o p q r s
t u v w x y z ! ?
1 2 3 4 5 6 7 8 9 0

ABCDEFGH
IJKLMNOP
QRSTUVWX
YZabcdefghi
jklmnopqrst
uvwxyz!?
1234567890